Welcome

If you are like many knitters, you started knitting by knitting for a baby. And like many knitters, you are still knitting for a baby. Instead of knitting for your own son or daughter, you are now knitting for your grand-children or the grandchild of your neighbor. Knitting for a baby is something you can do throughout your life. Once you knit the first piece, you will discover how relaxing, fun and easy it is to knit lovely baby items.

In this book you will find some great gift items that can be knit up quickly for a cute shower gift. We've also included several sweet blankets for a special little one. For those knitters who have a little more time, we have several baby layettes. Enjoy each stitch as you knit for baby!

Jeanne Stauffer, editor

Jeanne Stauffer

Table of Contents

Spa Baby Set,
page 20

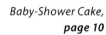

Baby-Shower Cake,
page 10

Soft Sunshine Blanket,
page 18

Easy Baby Booties

Designs by Frances Hughes

Skill Level

■□□□ BEGINNER

Finished Size

Foot: Approx 3½ inches long

Materials

- Sirdar Snuggly 55% nylon/45% acrylic DK weight yarn (191 yds/50g per ball): 1 ball petal pink #212 for pink bootie; 1 ball pastel blue #321 for blue bootie
- Size 2 (2.75mm) needles or size needed to obtain gauge
- 24 inches each pink and blue ⅛-inch-wide satin ribbon

Gauge

13 sts = 2 inches/5cm in St st.
To save time, take time to check gauge.

Special Abbreviation

Increase (inc): Knit in front and back of next st to inc 1 st.

Pink Bootie

Bottom

Cast on 40 sts.

Row 1 (RS): K1, inc, k16, inc, k2, inc, k16, inc, k1—44 sts.

Note: Mark Row 1 as RS row.

Row 2: Purl across.

Row 3: K1, inc, k18, inc, k2, inc, k18, inc, k1—48 sts.

Row 4: Purl across.

Row 5: K1, inc, k20, inc, k2, inc, k20, inc, k1—52 sts.

Rows 6–15: Beg with purl row, work in St st.

Shape Toe

Row 1 (WS): P30, p3tog, turn, leaving rem sts unworked.

Row 2 (RS): Sl 1k, k8, sl 1p, k2tog, psso, turn, leaving rem sts unworked.

Row 3: Sl 1p, p8, p3tog, turn, leaving rem sts unworked.

Rows 4–9: Rep [Rows 2 and 3] 3 times.

Row 10: Sl 1k, k8, sl 1p, k2tog, psso, knit rem sts—32 sts.

Cuff

Row 1 (WS): Purl across.

Row 2 (RS): Knit across.

Row 3 (eyelet row): P1, *yo, p2tog; rep from * across to last st, purl last st.

Row 4: Knit across.

Row 5: Purl across.

Row 6: Knit across.

Row 7: *K2tog, yo, [k1, yo] twice, [k2tog] twice; rep from * across.

Rows 8–15: Rep Rows 4–7.

Bind off knitwise. Cut yarn, leaving a long end for sewing.

Finishing

Sew back seam, then sew center bottom of sole. Cut ribbon in half and run length through eyelet row and tie in a bow.

Blue Bootie

Bottom

Cast on 40 sts.

Row 1 (RS): K1, inc, k16, inc, k2, inc, k16, inc, k1—44 sts.

Note: Mark Row 1 as RS row.

Row 2: Knit across.

Row 3: K1, inc, k18, inc, k2, inc, k18, inc, k1—48 sts.

Row 4: Knit across.

Row 5: K1, inc, k20, inc, k2, inc, k20, inc, k1—52 sts.

Rows 6–10: Knit across.

Rows 11–15: Work in St st.

continued on page 12

Dainty & Dapper Bibs

Designs by Dixie L. Butler

Skill Level
■□□□ BEGINNER

Dainty Bib

Finished Size
Approx 9 inches wide x 12½ inches long, including tabs

Materials
- Pisgah Yarn and Dyeing Co. Peaches & Crème 100% cotton worsted weight yarn (122 yds/2½ oz per ball): 1 ball each persimmon #33 (MC) and cream #3 (CC)
- Size 7 (4.5mm) needles or size needed to obtain gauge
- Stitch holder
- Tapestry needle
- 1 button (¾-inch diameter)

Gauge
17 sts and 24 rows = 4 inches/10cm in St st.
To save time, take time to check gauge.

Pattern Note
One ball of contrasting color yarn is sufficient for both the I-cord trim on the Dainty Bib and the bow tie on the Dapper Bib.

Lower Border
With MC, cast on 38 sts.

Knit 4 rows.

Eyelet row (WS): K2, *yo, k2tog, k2, rep from * across.

Knit 3 rows.

Body
Rows 1 (WS) and 3: K5, purl to last 5 sts, k5.

Row 2 (RS): K2, yo, k2tog, knit to last 3 sts, yo, k2tog, k1.

Row 4: Knit across.

Rep [Rows 1–4] until bib measures 7 inches.

Rep Row 1.

Knit 4 rows.

Neck
K10 sts and place on holder, bind off next 18 sts, knit rem sts.

Button tab
Work in garter st on 10 sts until tab measures 5 inches, ending by working a WS row.

Row 1 (RS): K2tog, knit to last 2 sts, k2tog—8 sts.

Row 2: Knit.

Rows 3 and 4: Rep Rows 1 and 2—6 sts.

Bind off.

Buttonhole tab
Sl sts from holder onto needle. With WS facing join yarn at neck edge. Work in garter st on 10 sts until tab measures 5 inches, ending by working a WS row.

Row 1 (RS): K2tog, knit to last 2 sts, k2tog—8 sts.

Row 2: Knit.

Row 3: K2tog, yo (for buttonhole), knit to last 4 sts, [k2tog] twice—6 sts.

Row 4: Knit.

Bind off.

I-cord trim
With CC, cast on 3 sts. *Sl sts onto LH needle, pulling yarn across back of work, k3; rep from * until I-cord measures about 24 inches. Sl st onto LH needle, k3tog.

Finishing
Lightly block bib. Referring to photo, weave I-cord through eyelet openings along edge of bib, adjusting length as necessary. Sew securely in place. Sew button on tab.

Dapper Bib

Finished Size
Approx 8½ inches wide x 12 inches long, including tab length

Materials

- Pisgah Yarn and Dyeing Co. Peaches & Crème 100% cotton worsted weight yarn (ombre: 98 yds/2 oz per ball; solid: 122 yds/2½ oz per ball): 1 ball each royal verde #174 (MC) and cream #3 (CC)
- Size 5 (3.75mm) needles or size needed to obtain gauge
- Stitch holder
- Tapestry needle
- 1 button (¾-inch diameter)

Gauge

18 sts and 26 rows = 4 inches/10cm in St st. To save time, take time to check gauge.

Special Abbreviation

Increase (inc): Knit in front and back of next st to inc 1 st.

Pattern Note

One ball of contrasting-color yarn is sufficient for both the I-cord trim on the Dainty Bib and the bow tie on the Dapper Bib.

Body

With MC, cast on 30 sts.

Rows 1 and 2: Knit.

Row 3 (RS): Inc, knit to last st, inc.

Row 4: K3, purl to last 3 sts, k3.

Rows 5–10: Rep [Rows 3 and 4] 3 times— 38 sts.

Row 11: Knit.

Row 12: K3, purl to last 3 sts, k3.

Rep Rows 11 and 12 until bib measures 7 inches from cast-on edge.

Neck

Row 1 (RS): Knit.

Row 2: K3, p3, knit to last 6 sts, p3, k3.

Row 3: K9 and place on holder, bind off next 20 sts, knit rem sts.

Button tab

Row 1: K3, p3, k3.

Row 2: K9.

Rep Rows 1 and 2 until tab measures 5 inches.

Knit 2 rows.

Bind off.

continued on page 14

Baby Hat Quartet

Designs by Michele P. Wilcox

Skill Level
■■☐☐ EASY

Size
6–12 months

Finished Measurements
Circumference: 12 inches
Height: Yellow, Lavender and Blue & White Hats:
Approx 6 inches; Stocking Hat: Approx 9½ inches

Materials
- **Yellow Hat:** Red Heart Kids 100% acrylic worsted weight yarn (290 yds/141g per skein): 1 skein yellow #2230 【4 MEDIUM】
- **Lavender Hat:** Red Heart Baby Econo 100% acrylic worsted weight yarn (675 yds/198g per skein): 1 skein lavender #1570
- **Blue & White Hat:** Bernat Softee Baby 100% acrylic DK weight yarn (468 yds/140g per ball): 1 ball pale blue #02002, small amount white #02000 【3 LIGHT】
- **Stocking Hat:** Moda Dea Sassy Stripes 100% acrylic DK weight yarn (147 yds/50g per ball): 1 ball crayon #6250
- Size 5 (3.75mm) needles or size needed to obtain gauge
- Tapestry needle

Gauge
Yellow, Blue & White and Stocking Hats: 24 sts and 30 rows = 4 inches/10cm in St st.
Lavender Hat: 21 sts and 36 rows = 4 inches/10cm in Lace pat.
To save time, take time to check gauge.

Pattern Stitches
Lace (multiple of 3 sts)
Row 1: *K1, yo, k2tog; rep from * across.
Rep Row 1 for pat.

Stripe
Row 1: With blue knit across.
Row 2: Purl across.
Rows 3 and 4: Rep Rows 1 and 2.
Rows 5 and 6: With white, knit across.
Rep Rows 1–6 for pat.

Yellow Hat
With yellow, cast on 72 sts.

Work even in St st until hat measures 5¾ inch from beg. (Unroll natural curl of cuff to measure)

Shape top
Row 1: [K7, k2tog] across—64 sts.

Row 2 and all even rows: Purl.

Row 3: [K6, k2tog] across—56 sts.

Row 5: [K5, k2tog] across—48 sts.

Row 7: [K4, k2tog] across—40 sts.

Row 9: [K3, k2tog] across—32 sts.

Row 11: [K2 k2tog] across—24 sts.

Row 13: [K1, k2tog] across—16 sts.

Row 15: [K2tog] across—8 sts.

Topknot
Work rem 8 sts in St st for 3½ inches.

Cut yarn, leaving an 18-inch end, draw through sts on needle twice. Sew back seam, including topknot.

Tie a knot in the tip of hat.

Lavender Hat
With lavender, cast on 72 sts.

Work in k2, p2 ribbing for 1 inch.

Change to Lace pat and work even until hat measures 4¾ inches from beg.

Shape top
Row 1: *Work 18 sts in pat, [k2tog] 3 times; rep from * across—63 sts.

Row 2: Work even in pat.

Row 3: Work 15 sts in pat, [k2tog] 3 times, work 21 sts in pat, [k2tog] 3 times, work 15 sts in pat—57 sts.

Row 4: Work even in pat.

Row 5: *Work 12 sts in pat, [k2tog] 3 times; rep from * across, ending last 3 sts in pat—48 sts.

Row 6: Work even in pat.

Row 7: [K2, k2tog] across—36 sts.

Row 8: Purl across.

Row 9: [K1, k2tog] across—24 sts.

Row 10: Purl across.

Row 11: [K2tog] across—12 sts.

Cut yarn, leaving an 18-inch length.

Thread yarn needle and draw through rem sts twice, pulling tightly to secure. Sew back seam.

Pompom
Make small pompom by wrapping yarn 40 times around a 2-inch piece of cardboard. Tie length of yarn around loops at one end. Cut other end and trim ends. Sew to top of hat.

Blue & White Hat
With blue, cast on 72 sts.

Work in k1, p1 ribbing for ¾ inch.

Work in Stripe pat for 24 rows. Change to white.

Shape top
Row 1: [K7, k2tog] across—64 sts.

Row 2: Knit across, change to blue.

Row 3: [K6, k2tog] across—56 sts.

Row 4: Purl across.

Row 5: [K5, k2tog] across—48 sts.

Row 6: Purl across, change to white.

Row 7: [K4, k2tog] across—40 sts.

Row 8: Knit across, change to blue.

Work remainder of hat in St st with blue.

Row 9: [K3, k2tog] across—32 sts.

Row 10: Purl across.

Row 11: [K2, k2tog] across—24 sts.

Row 12: Purl across.

Row 13: [K1, k2tog] across—16 sts.

Row 14: Purl across.

Row 15: [K2tog] across—8 sts.

Rows 16–21: Work even in St st.

Cut yarn, leaving an 18-inch end.

Thread yarn needle and draw yarn through rem sts twice, pulling tightly to secure. Sew back seam including tip.

Turn up cuff.

Stocking Hat
With crayon, cast on 72 sts.

Work in k1, p1 ribbing for 1 inch.

Work even in St st until hat measures 4¾ inches, ending with a WS row.

Shape top
Row 1: [K7, k2tog] across—64 sts.

Row 2: Purl across.

Rows 3–6: Work even in St st.

Row 7: [K6, k2tog] across—56 sts.

Rows 8–12: Rep Rows 2–6.

Row 13: [K5, k2tog] across—48 sts.

Rows 14–18: Rep Rows 2–6.

Row 19: [K4, k2tog] across—40 sts.

Rows 20–24: Rep Rows 2–6.

Row 25: [K3, k2tog] across—32 sts.

Rows 26–30: Rep Rows 2–6.

Row 31: [K2, k2tog] across—24 sts.

Rows 32–36: Rep Rows 2–6.

Row 37: [K1, k2tog] across—16 sts.

Row 38: Purl across.

Row 39: [K2tog] across—8 sts.

Cut yarn, leaving an 18-inch end.

Thread yarn needle and draw through rem sts twice, pulling tightly to secure. Sew back seam.

Tassel
Wrap yarn 30 times around a 2½-inch piece of cardboard. With length of yarn, tie loops tightly at one end. Cut other end.

With another length of yarn wrap and tie tassel again, about ¾ inch below first tie. Attach tassel to top of hat. ❖

Baby-Shower Cake

Designs by Lainie Hering

Skill Level

■□□□ BEGINNER

Finished Sizes

Washcloths: Approx 7 x 8 inches
Burp Cloth: Approx 6 x 12 inches
Cake Roll: Approx 3½ inches high x 4½ inches across

Materials

- Lily Sugar'n Cream 100% cotton worsted weight yarn (120 yds/56g per ball): 1 ball each sunshine #00073 and white #00001
- Size 7 needles or size needed to obtain gauge
- ½ yd ½- to ¾-inch-wide ribbon
- Small purchased rubber duck toy
- Yellow baby safety pins (optional)

Gauge

20 sts = 4 inches/10cm in St st.
To save time, take time to check gauge.

White Washcloth

With white, cast on 36 sts.

Knit 2 rows.

Set up pat

Row 1 (RS): Knit across.

Row 2: Purl across.

Rows 3 and 4: Rep Rows 1 and 2.

Rows 5 and 6: Knit.

Rep [Rows 1–6] 7 times.

Bind off.

Yellow Washcloth

With sunshine, cast on 36 sts.

Rows 1 and 2: *K1, p1; rep from * across.

Rows 3 and 4: *P1, k1; rep from across.

Rep Rows 1–4 until piece measures 7 inches.

Bind off in pat.

Burp Cloth

With sunshine, cast on 35 sts.

Row 1: *K2, p2; rep from * to last 3 sts, end k2, p1.

Rep Row 1 until piece measures 12 inches.

Bind off in pat.

Cake Roll

Fold each of the 3 cloths in half with the fold being placed on the longest side. Wrap the washcloths in jelly-roll fashion, then wrap burp cloth around outside of roll. Wrap ribbon around "cake roll." Tape closed, or secure with fabric glue. Use safety pins if needed to hold corners of outer cloth to the roll. Secure toy duck with tape to top of cake (folded edges up). ❖

Rainbow Car-Seat Blanket

Design by Kennita Tully

Skill Level
 ■■■□ INTERMEDIATE

Finished Sizes
Blanket: Approx 36 inches square
Car-Seat Cover-Up: Approx 24 inches square

Materials
- Plymouth Dreambaby DK 50% microfiber acrylic/50% nylon DK weight yarn (183 yds/50g per ball): 11 balls bright multi #210 for Blanket; 5 balls bright multi #210 for Car-Seat Cover-Up
- Size 6 (4.25mm) 36–40 inch circular needle or size needed to obtain gauge
- Tapestry needle

Gauge
17 sts and 39 rows = 4 inches/10cm in pat st.
To save time, take time to check gauge.

Pattern Stitch
Reversible St (worked over an odd number of sts)

Row 1: K2, *yo, k1; rep from * to last st, end p1.

Row 2: K1, purl across.

Rows 3: K2, [k2tog] to last st, end p1.

Rows 4 and 5: K2, *yo, k2 tog; rep from * to last st, end p1.

Rows 6 and 7: Knit to last st, p1.

Rep Rows 1–7 for pat.

Pattern Notes
Instructions are given for Car-Seat Cover-Up with changes for larger blanket in parentheses. This pattern is reversible, so no right or wrong side is indicated.

Blanket
Cast on 101 (153) sts.

Knit 2 rows.

Beg with Row 1, work Reversible St pat until piece measures approx 24 (36) inches or desired length ending with Row 7.

Bind off all sts.

Finishing
Weave in all ends. Wash and pin to measurements. ❖

Easy Baby Booties

Continued from page 2

Shape Toe
Row 1 (WS): P30, p3tog, turn, leaving rem sts unworked.

Row 2 (RS): Sl 1k, k8, sl 1p, k2tog, psso, turn, leaving rem sts unworked.

Row 3: Sl 1p, p8, p3tog, turn, leaving rem sts unworked.

Rows 4–9: Rep [Rows 2 and 3] 3 times.

Row 10: Sl 1k, k8, sl 1p, k2tog, psso, knit rem sts—32 sts.

Cuff
Row 1 (WS): Purl across.

Row 2 (RS): Knit across.

Row 3 (eyelet row): P1, *yo, p2tog; rep from * to last st, purl last st.

Row 4–7: Work in St st.

Row 8–12: [K1, p1] across.

Bind off in rib pat.

Finishing
Sew back seam, then sew center bottom of sole. Cut ribbon in half and run length through eyelet row and tie in a bow. ❖

Textured Squares

Design by Melissa Leapman

Skill Level
◼◼◻◻ **EASY**

Finished Size
Approx 35 x 45 inches

Materials
- Caron Simply Soft Brites 100% acrylic worsted weight yarn (315 yds/6 oz per skein): 5 skeins grape #9610
- Size 7 (4.5mm) circular needle
- Size 9 (5.5mm) circular needle or size needed to obtain gauge

Gauge
18 sts and 24 rows = 4 inches/10cm in pat on larger needles.
To save time, take time to check gauge.

Pattern Note
Circular needles are used in order to accommodate the large number of stitches. Do not join; work back and forth in rows.

Afghan
With smaller needle, cast on 159 sts.

Work 6 rows of garter st—3 ridges.

Change to larger needle.

Set up pat

Row 1 (RS): K12, *p1, k1, p1, k9; rep from * across, ending k3.

Row 2: K3, *p9, k3; rep from * across.

Rows 3–10: Rep [Rows 1 and 2] 4 times.

Row 11: Rep Row 1.

Row 12: Knit across.

Row 13: K4, *p1, k1; rep from * across, ending k3.

Row 14: Knit across.

Rep Rows 1–14 until afghan measures approx 44 inches from beg, ending with Row 10.

Change to smaller needle and work 6 rows in garter st.

Bind off all sts. Weave in ends. ❖

Dainty & Dapper Bibs

Continued from page 6

Buttonhole tab
Sl sts from holder onto needle. With WS facing attach yarn at neck edge.

Row 1 (WS): K3, p3, k3.

Row 2 (RS): K9.

Rep Rows 1 and 2 until tab measures 4½ inches, ending with a WS row.

Shape top
Row 1: K3, yo (for buttonhole), k2tog, k4.

Row 2: K3, p3, k3.

Row 3: Knit.

Row 4: Rep Row 2.

Knit 3 rows.

Bind off all sts.

Bow Tie
With CC, cast on 12 sts, knit 14 rows—7 ridges.

Bind off all sts.

Referring to photo, wrap a strand of CC yarn around center of piece and tie tightly to form bow tie. Sew on bib.

Lightly block bib, sew button to tab. ❖

Ruffled Blocks Baby Blanket

Design by Dawn Brocco

Skill Level

■■■□ INTERMEDIATE

Finished Size

Approx 38 x 49 inches, including ruffled edge

Materials

- Plymouth Wildflower D.K. 51% cotton/49% acrylic DK weight yarn (136 yds/50g per ball): 24 balls ecru #40
- Size 8 (5.mm) 24- or 29-inch circular needles and 2 double-pointed needles or size needed to obtain gauge
- Cable needle
- Stitch holder
- Tapestry needle

Gauge

16 sts and 24 rows = 4 inches/10cm in St st, using 2 strands of yarn.
To save time, take time to check gauge.

Special Abbreviations

Crossed Twist (CT): Sl next 3 sts to cable needle and hold in back, knit next st, sl 2 sts from cable needle to LH needle, bring cable needle with rem st to front, k2 from LH needle, knit st from cable needle.
Wrap/Turn (W/T): Sl next st from left to right needle, bring yarn to front between needles, return slipped st to LH needle, turn work.

Pattern Stitches

Crossed-St Block
Row 1 (RS): Knit.
Row 2: *K2, p6; rep from * across to last 2 sts, k2.
Rows 3–8: Rep [Rows 1 and 2] 3 times.
Row 9: K7, *sl 1p, k2, sl 1p, k4; rep from * across to last 3 sts, k3.
Row 10: K7, *sl 1p wyif, k2, sl 1p wyif, k4; rep from * across to last 3 sts, k3.
Rows 11 and 12: Rep Rows 9 and 10.
Row 13: K7, *CT, k4; rep from * across to last 3 sts, k3.
Row 14: Rep Row 2.
Rep Rows 1–14 for pat.

Welted Ruffle
Note: W/T is used to work short rows on Rows 2 and 5.
Row 1: Knit.
Row 2: P10, W/T, k10.
Row 3: P10, k3.
Row 4: K3, p10.
Row 5: K10, W/T, p10.
Row 6: Knit.
Rep Rows 1–6 for pat.

Pattern Notes

Blanket is worked using 2 strands of yarn worked together throughout.
Ruffled edge is worked separately, then sewn on afterward.

Blanket

With 2 strands yarn, cast on 130 sts.

Rows 1–252: Work [Rows 1–14 of Crossed-St Block pat] 18 times.

Rows 253–260: Rep Rows 1–8.

Bind off as to knit.

Ruffle Edging

Cast on 13 sts. Work Welted Ruffle pat back and forth on dpns until 219 ruffles (438 garter rows on welt or short edge) are completed, do not bind off, sl sts to a holder.

Finishing

Lay blanket flat with RS facing. Using 1 strand of yarn and tapestry needle, beg at upper LH corner of long edge of blanket, attach ruffle edging to blanket using overcast st, matching garter ridges of blanket to garter ridges of welt on ruffle edging. At each corner, ease 2 or 3 garter welt ridges around edge to relieve puckering.

On short sides of the blanket, before sewing tog, pin 4 welt garter ridges to each 6 sts of blanket pat. As you come to starting point, knit additional reps of welt pat, if necessary. Bind off as to purl.

Sew ends of ruffle edging tog. Weave in all ends. ❖

Soft Sunshine Baby Blanket

Design by Lorraine White

Skill Level

■■□□ EASY

Finished Size

Approx 30 x 35 inches, excluding fringe

Materials

- NaturallyCaron.com Country 75% microdenier acrylic/25% merino wool worsted weight yarn (185 yds/85g per skein): 5 skeins soft sunshine #0003
- Size 9 (5.25mm) needles or size needed to obtain gauge
- Cable needle
- Stitch markers

Gauge

16 sts and 24 rows = 4 inches/10cm in St st.
To save time, take time to check gauge.

Special Abbreviation

Cable Back (CB): Sl next 3 sts to cn and hold in back of work, k3, k3 from cn.

Pattern Stitches

Moss St (multiple of 2 sts)
Row 1: [K1, p1] across.
Row 2: Knit the purl sts and purl the knit sts across.
Rep Row 2 for pat.

Cable (worked over 10 sts)
Row 1 (RS): P2, k6, p2
Row 2: K2, p6, k2
Rows 3–6: Rep [Rows 1 and 2] twice.
Row 7: P2, CB, p2.
Row 8: Rep Row 2.
Rep Rows 1–8 for pat.

Ridge (worked over 10 sts)
Row 1 (RS): K10.
Row 2: P10.
Rows 3–6: Rep [Rows 1 and 2] twice.
Row 7: P10.
Row 8: Rep Row 2.
Rep Rows 1–8 for pat.

Blanket

Note: *Knit the first and last st of each row for edge st throughout entire blanket.*

Cast on 138 sts.

Lower Border

Row 1: K1 for edge st, work in Moss St pat to last st, k1 for edge st.

Rows 2–12: Rep Row 1.

Body

K1, work Moss St pat as established over next 10 sts, place marker, work Cable pat over next 10 sts, place marker, work Ridge pat over next 10 sts, place marker, work Cable pat over next 10 sts, place marker, work Moss St pat as established over next 12 sts, place marker, [work Cable pat over 10 sts, k1] twice, work Cable pat over next 10 sts, place marker, work Moss St pat as established over next 12 sts, place marker, work Cable pat over next 10 sts, place marker, work Ridge pat over next 10 sts, place marker, work Cable pat over next 10 sts, place marker, work Moss St pat as established over next 10 sts, k1.

Continue working even in pats as established working single sts between center cables in St st.

Work even in established pats until blanket measures approx 33½ inches from beg, ending with Row 8 of Cable and Ridge pats.

Work 12 rows in Moss St pat, continuing to knit the first and last sts.

Bind off in pat and weave in all ends.

Fringe

Cut yarn in 10-inch lengths. Using 2 strands for each knot, tie knots in every 3rd st along top and bottom edges of blanket. Trim ends even. ❖

Spa Baby Set

Designs by Barb Bettegnies

Skill Level
■■□□ EASY

Size
12 months

Finished Measurements
Chest: 24 inches
Hat: 16 inches in circumference
Sock Foot: Approx 4 inches long

Materials
- NaturallyCaron.com Spa 75% microdenier acrylic/25% bamboo DK weight yarn (251 yds/85g per skein): 1 skein each green sheen #0004 (A), naturally #0007 (B), coral lipstick #0002 (C), soft sunshine #0003 (D) and ocean spray #0005 (E)
- Size 5 (3.75mm) knitting needles
- Size 6 (4.25mm) knitting needles or size needed to obtain gauge
- Stitch holders

Gauge
25 sts and 28 rows = 4 inches/10cm in Yarn Over pat. To save time, take time to check gauge.

Pattern Stitch
Yarn Over
Row 1: *Yo, k2, pass yo over 2 knit sts; rep from * across.
Row 2: Purl across.

Pattern Notes
Yarn amounts are sufficient for entire set.

Vest is made in one piece to underarms, and then divided for fronts and back.

Four stitches are worked in garter stitch (knit every row) at edges for center front and armhole border. Wind two 6-yard lengths of A for front edges and four 4-yard lengths of A for vest armhole edges.

Bring new color under color just used each time you reach markers (intarsia method).
All pieces are worked flat.

Vest Sweater
With smaller needles and A, cast on 136 sts.

Lower Border
Rows 1–7: Knit.

Change to larger needles.

Body
Row 1 (RS): K4, place marker, work Row 1 of Yarn Over pat to last 4 sts, place marker, k4.

Row 2: K4, work Row 2 of Yarn Over pat to last 4 sts, k4.

Rows 3–12: Continue in pat as established, working first and last 4 sts in garter st (knit every row) and rem sts in Yarn Over pat.

Rows 13–16: With A knit first and last 4 sts, attach B and knit rem sts. Fasten off B.

Rows 17–28: With A knit first and last 4 sts, attach C and work Yarn Over pat over rem sts. Fasten off C.

Rows 28–32: With A knit first and last 4 sts, attach B and knit rem sts. Fasten off B.

Right Front
Row 1 (RS): K4A, attach D, work in Yarn Over pat across next 28 sts, attach a shorter length of A, k4A—36 sts (28D, 8A).

Turn.

Note: Rem sts may be left on needle or placed on holder.

Rows 2–12: Continue in pat as established, working first and last 4 sts in garter st and rem sts in Yarn Over pat with D. Fasten off D.

Rows 13–16: With A knit first and last 4 sts, attach B and knit rem sts. Fasten off B.

Neck shaping
Row 17 (RS): Place first 10 sts on st holder (4A, 6B sts), attach E and work Yarn Over pat across next 22 sts, k4A edge sts—26 sts (22E, 4A).

Rows 18–24: Continue in pat as established, bind off 2 sts at neck edge [every RS row] 3 times—20 sts (16E, 4A).

Rows 25–28: Continue even in pat as established. Fasten off E.

Rows 29–32: Maintaining garter st border with A, attach B and knit rem sts.

Place sts on holder for shoulder.

Back
Row 1 (RS): With RS facing, attach a short length of A and knit next 4 sts, attach D and work Yarn Over pat across next 56 sts, attach a short length of A and knit next 4 sts—64 sts (56D, 8A).

Turn, leaving rem sts on needle or holder.

Rows 2–12: Continue in pat as established working first and last 4 sts in garter st with A and rem sts in Yarn Over pat with D. Fasten off D.

Rows 13–16: With A knit first and last 4 sts, attach B and knit center 56 sts. Fasten off B.

Rows 17–28: With A knit first and last 4 sts, attach E and work rem sts in Yarn Over pat. Fasten off E.

Rows 29–31: With A knit first and last 4 sts, attach B and knit rem sts.

Row 32: K4A, k15B, k2tog and place these 20 sts on holder for shoulder, bind off next 22 sts, ssk, knit rem sts and place these 20 sts on holder for shoulder.

Left Front
Row 1 (RS): Attach a shorter length of A and knit next 4 sts, attach D, work Yarn Over pat across next 28 sts, attach a shorter length of A and knit next 4 sts—36 sts (28D, 8A).

Rows 2–12: Continue in pat as established, working first and last 4 sts in garter st with A, and rem sts in Yarn Over pat with D. Fasten off D.

Rows 13–16: With A knit first and last 4 sts, attach B and knit rem sts. Fasten off B.

Neck shaping
Row 17 (RS): K4A, attach E and work Yarn Over pat across next 22 sts, place rem 10 sts (6B, 4A sts) on st holder—26 sts (22E, 4A).

Rows 18–24: Continue in pat as established, binding off 2 sts at neck edge [every WS row] 3 times—20 sts (16E, 4A).

Rows 25–28: Continue even in pat as established. Fasten off E.

Rows 29–32: Maintaining garter st border with A, attach B and knit rem sts.

Place sts on holder for shoulder.

Assembly
With B and spare needle, seam shoulders using 3-needle bind off.

Neckband
With A and smaller needle, with RS facing knit 10 sts from front right holder, pick up and knit 12 sts along right front neck edge to seam, k22 sts across back neck edge, pick up and knit 12 sts along left front neck edge, knit 10 sts from left front holder. 22 from left front—66 sts.

Rows 1 and 2: Knit across.

Row 3 (buttonhole row): K2, yo, k2tog, knit across.

Rows 4–6: Knit across.

Bind off.

I-cord tie
With smaller needle and C cast on 4 sts. *Sl sts back to LH needle, pulling yarn across back, k4; rep from * until I-cord measures 6 inches. Pull yarn across back and bind off. Finish off.

Referring to photo, attach center of I-cord to left front opposite buttonhole.

Hat
Body
With smaller needles and A, cast on 90 sts.

Rows 1–8: Knit across.

Change to larger needles.

Rows 9–16: Rep [Rows 1 and 2 of Yarn Over pat] 4 times. Fasten off A.

Rows 17 and 18: With B, knit. Fasten off B.

Rows 19–26: Attach C and rep [Rows 1 and 2 of Yarn Over pat] 4 times. Fasten off C.

Rows 27 and 28: Rep Rows 17 and 18.

Rows 29–36: Attach D and rep [Rows 1 and 2 of Yarn Over pat] 4 times. Fasten off D.

Rows 37 and 38: Rep Rows 17 and 18.

Change to smaller needles.

Shape crown
Row 1: Attach E, *yo, k1, k2tog, pass yo over last 2 sts; rep from * across—60 sts.

Row 2: Purl across.

Rows 3 and 4: Rep Rows 1 and 2—40 sts.

Row 5: *Yo, k1, k2tog, pass yo over last 2 sts; rep from * across to last st, k1—27 sts.

Row 6: Purl across.

Rows 7–10: Rep [Rows 1 and 2] twice—12 sts.

Place sts on holder.

Seam hat and weave ends.

I-cord tassel
Place 4 sts from holder onto smaller needle. Attach A, *sl sts onto LH needle, pulling yarn across back, k4; rep from * until I-cord measures 3 inches. Pull yarn across back and bind off. Weave in ends.

Rep with rem sts, working with 4 sts at a time.

Tighten base of I-cords tog.

Socks
Cuff
With smaller needles and A, cast on 30 sts.

Rows 1–5: Knit across. Fasten off A.

Change to larger needles.

Rows 6 (RS)–9: Attach E, work [Rows 1 and 2 of Yarn Over pat] twice. Fasten off E.

Rows 10 and 11: With B; knit.

Note: Do not cut B; carry yarn loosely along side of work.

Rows 12–15: Attach D, work [Rows 1 and 2 of Yarn Over pat] twice. Fasten off D.

Rows 16 and 17: Rep Rows 10 and 11.

Rows 18–21: Attach C; work [Rows 1 and 2 of Yarn Over pat] twice. Fasten off C.

Rows 22 and 23: Rep Rows 10 and 11. Fasten off B.

Instep
With A, k20. Turn, leaving rem 10 sts unworked. K10, for instep, turn, leaving rem 10 sts unworked.

Working on 10 instep sts only knit 18 more rows—10 ridges.

Toe shaping
Pick up and knit 10 sts along left edge of instep, knit 10 unworked sts. Turn. Knit 30 sts. Pick up and purl 10 sts along right edge of instep, knit 10 rem unworked sts—50 sts.

Foot
Rows 1 and 2: Knit across.

Row 3: K1, k2tog, k20, [k2tog] twice, k20, k2tog, k1—46 sts.

Row 4: Knit across.

Row 5: K1, k2tog, k18, [k2tog] twice, k18, k2tog, k1—42 sts.

Row 6: Knit across.

Row 7: K1, k2tog, k16, [k2tog] twice, k16, k2tog, k1—38 sts.

Row 8: Knit across.

K19, place 2 needles parallel with RS tog, with spare needle seam sole using 3-needle bind off. Fasten off, leaving 10-inch tail for sewing.

Finishing
Sew back seam and weave in ends. ❖

Precious Baby Set

Designs by Lainie Hering

Skill Level

 ■■□□ EASY

Sizes

Infant: Newborn–6 months (6–12 months) Instructions are given for smaller size, with larger size in parentheses. When only 1 number is given, it applies to both sizes.

Finished Measurements

Chest: 20 (22) inches, buttoned
Hat: 12½ (14) inches in circumference

Materials

- Red Heart Designer Sport 100% acrylic DK weight yarn (279 yds/85g per ball): 2 balls ivory #3101 (MC) and 1 ball blossom #3701 *or* Dutch blue #3815 (CC)
- Size 6 (4.25mm) straight needles
- Size 7 (4.5mm) 24- to 29-inch circular needle or size needed to obtain gauge
- 3 buttons (½-inch diameter)
- 1 yd ¼-inch-wide ribbon
- Stitch holders
- Stitch markers
- Tapestry needle

Gauge

20 sts and 24 rows = 4 inches/10cm in St st on larger needle.
To save time, take time to check gauge.

Pattern Notes

Yarn amounts are sufficient for entire layette.

The sweater is knit from the neck down.

All wrong side purl rows begin and end with knit 4 stitches to form garter stitch buttonhole bands.

Circular needle is used to accommodate stitches, do not join. Work back and forth in rows.

Sweater

Neck edge

With larger needles and CC cast on 46 (50) sts.

Drop CC. Join MC. Knit 2 rows.

Set-up pat

Row 1 (inc row): K9 (10) for left front; yo, k1 for seam st; yo, k3 for sleeve; yo, k1 for seam st; yo, k18 (20) for back; yo, k1 for seam st; yo, k3 for sleeve; yo, k1 for seam st; yo, k9 (10) for right front—54 (58) sts.

Row 2: K4, purl across row to last 4 sts, k4.

Note: For Buttonhole: On boy's sweater, place buttonhole on left side by working k2, yo, k2tog work rem sts in established pat. On the next row, knit the yo for buttonhole. On girl's sweater, place buttonhole on right side by working in pat as established to last 4 sts, k2tog, yo, k2. On the next row, knit the yo for buttonhole.

Rep [Rows 1 and 2] 12 (13) times, and *at the same time,* on 2nd inc row (RS) make the 1st buttonhole. Rep buttonhole [every 2 inches] twice—3 buttonholes.

Note: 3rd buttonhole is worked after sts are divided for body.

Divide for Body

Place sts for body on separate st holders as follows:

Place 22 (24) sts from left front on a holder, 31 (33) sts including 2 seam sts from left sleeve on a holder, 44 (48) sts from back on a holder, 31 (33) sts including 2 seam sts from right sleeve on a holder and 22 (24) sts from right front on a holder.

Sleeves

Place left sleeve sts on needle. With RS facing and MC, cast on 2 sts and knit across.

Next row: Cast on 2 sts and purl across.

Work in St st for 2½ (3) inches.

Next row: Continue in St st dec 1 st at each end.

Continue in St st until sleeve measures 4½ (6) inches, ending by working a RS row.

Next row: Continue in St st dec 1 st on each end of row. Cut MC.

Join CC, knit 2 rows.

Bind off loosely.

Rep for right sleeve.

Body

Sl left front, back and right front sts onto needle. Attach MC.

Next row (RS): Knit across left front sts, pick up and knit 4 sts across cast-on sts at sleeve underarm, knit across back, pick up and knit 4 sts across other sleeve underarm, knit across rem front.

Work in St st, maintaining in garter st border and working rem buttonhole as indicated, until body measures 4 (5) inches, ending with WS.

Work 10 rows of garter st as follows:

With CC, knit 2 rows.

With MC, knit 2 rows.

With CC, knit 2 rows.

With MC, knit 2 rows.

Bind off.

Finishing

Block sweater gently with iron, placing a cloth over piece.

Sew sleeve seams; sew on buttons.

Hat

With CC and larger needle, cast on 64 (72) sts.

Knit 2 rows. Drop CC.

Join MC and knit 2 rows. Work in St st for 2½ (3½) inches.

Continuing in St st, work 2 rows with CC, 2 rows with MC and 2 rows with CC. Drop CC.

Join MC.

Shape crown

Row 1: *K6, k2tog; rep from * across—56 (64) sts.

Row 2 and all even rows: Purl.

Row 3: *K5, k2tog; rep from * across—48 (56) sts.

Row 5: *K4, k2tog; rep from * across—40 (48) sts.

Row 7: *K3, k2tog; rep from * across—32 (40) sts.

Row 9: *K2, k2tog; rep from * across—24 (32) sts.

Rows 11, 13: K2tog across—6 (8) sts.

Cut yarn leaving long tail. With tapestry needle thread tail through rem sts. Pull to tighten. Sew back seam.

Make small pompom using MC and CC tog. Fasten securely to top of hat.

Optional Earflaps

Mark st 1½ (2) inches on each side of back seam. Beg at 1 marked st, with MC pick up and knit 12 (14) sts working toward front of hat.

Knit 10 (12) rows.

Next row: K2tog, knit to last 2 sts, k2tog.

Rep last row until 2 sts rem.

K2tog, cut yarn and pull through last st. Weave in ends.

Rep on opposite side for 2nd earflap.

Booties

Note: Bootie size is determined by needle size. Instructions are the same for both sizes.

With smaller (larger) needle and CC, cast on 32 sts.

Knit 2 rows. Drop CC

Change to MC and knit 11 rows.

Next row (WS): P14, place marker, p4, place marker, p14.

Shape foot

Row 1: Knit to st before marker, inc, k1, sl marker, knit to next marker, sl marker, k1, inc, knit to end of row.

Row 2: Purl across.

Rep Rows 1 and 2 until there are 44 sts on needle ending with a purl row.

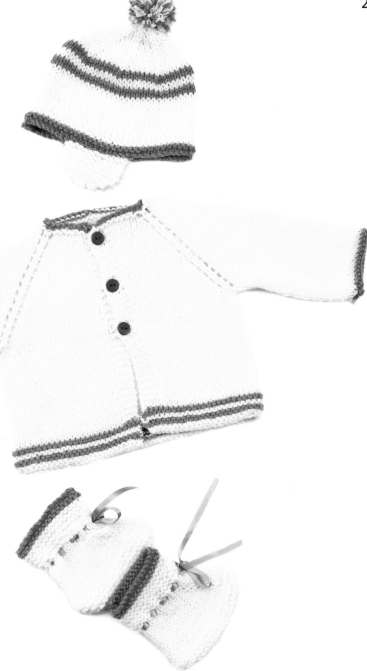

Knit 10 rows.

Bind off loosely.

Finishing

Sew sole and back seam of bootie.

Cut ribbon into two 18-inch lengths. Referring to photo, weave ribbon with tapestry needle through row below garter st ankle cuff, beg and ending at midpoint of toe, and weaving over and under evenly around the bottom of cuff. Tie ribbon in bow at front. ❖

Baby Cable Layette

Designs by Lisa Carnahan

Skill Level

■■■□ INTERMEDIATE

Sizes

Fits newborn—1 year
Instructions are given for smallest size with larger sizes (size) given in parentheses. When only 1 number is given, it applies to all (both) sizes.

Finished Measurements

Chest: 18 (20, 22, 24) inches
Head: 12 (16) inches in circumference
Foot: 3½ (4½) inches long

Materials

- Plymouth Dreambaby DK 50% microfiber acrylic/50% nylon DK weight yarn (183 yds/50g per ball): 2 (3, 3, 4) balls blue #124 for Sweater; 1 (1) ball blue #124 for Hat; 1 (1) ball blue #124 for Booties; 5 (9) balls blue #124 for Blanket
- Size 3 (3.25mm) straight and 16-inch circular needles (for neckband and hat)
- Size 5 (3.75mm) straight, 16-inch circular (for hat) and double-pointed needles (for hat) or size needed to obtain gauge
- Stitch holders
- Cable needle
- Stitch marker
- Tapestry needle

Gauge

22 sts and 32 rows = 4 inches/10cm in St st with larger needles.
To save time, take time to check gauge.

Special Abbreviations

Cable 4 Back (C4B): Sl next 2 sts to cable needle, hold in back, k2, k2 from cable needle.

Cable 6 Back (C6B): Sl next 3 sts to cable needle, hold in back, k3, k3 from cable needle.

Purl 2 together through back loops (p2tog-tbl): Purl next 2 sts tog through the back loops.

Ssk (slip, slip, knit): Sl next 2 sts, one at a time, as if to knit. Insert LH needle through front of sts and knit these 2 sts tog.

Sweater

Back

With smaller needle, cast on 64 (70, 76, 82) sts.

Row 1 (WS): K6 (7, 8, 9), *p4, k8 (9, 10, 11); rep from * 3 more times, p4, k6 (7, 8, 9).

Row 2 (RS): K5 (6, 7, 8), *p1, k4, p1, k6 (7, 8, 9); rep from * 3 more times, p1, k4, p1, k5 (6, 7, 8).

Rows 3 and 4: Rep Rows 1 and 2.

Row 5: Rep Row 1.

Row 6: K5 (6, 7, 8), *p1, C4B, p1, k6 (7, 8, 9); rep from * 3 more times, p1, C4B, p1, k5 (6, 7, 8).

Rows 7 and 8: Rep Rows 1 and 2.

Row 9: Rep Row 1.

Change to larger needles.

Work pat as follows:

Row 1 (RS): K5 (6, 7, 8), *p1, k4, p1, k6 (7, 8, 9); rep from * 3 more times, p1, k4, p1, k5 (6, 7, 8).

Row 2: P5 (6, 7, 8), *k1, p4, k1, p6 (7, 8, 9); rep from * 3 more times, k1, p4, k1, p5 (6, 7, 8).

Row 3: K5 (6, 7, 8), *p1, C4B, p1, k6 (7, 8, 9); rep from * 3 more times, p1, C4B, p1, k5 (6, 7, 8).

Row 4: Rep Row 2.

Row 5: Rep Row 1.

Row 6: K6 (7, 8, 9), *p4, k8, (9, 10, 11); rep from * 3 more times, p4, k6 (7, 8, 9).

Rep Rows 1–6 until piece measures 8½ (9½, 10½, 11½) inches.

Shape neck

Work in pattern across 18 (20, 22, 24) sts. Place next 28 (30, 32, 34) sts on st holder. Join a 2nd ball of yarn and work across rem 18 (20, 22, 24) sts.

Working both sides at once with separate balls of yarn, work even in pat until piece measures 9 (10, 11, 12) inches.

Bind off all sts.

Front

Work same as back until piece measures 7½ (8½, 9½, 10½) inches.

Shape neck

Work in pat across 24 (26, 28, 30) sts. Place next 16 (18, 20, 22) sts on st holder. Join 2nd ball of yarn and work in pat across rem 24 (26, 28, 30) sts.

Working both shoulders at once with separate balls of yarn at neck edge, bind off 3 sts, then bind off 2 sts, then bind off 1 st—18 (20, 22, 24) sts on each shoulder.

Work even until piece measures 9 (10, 11, 12) inches.

Bind off all sts.

Sleeves

Cuff

With smaller needle, cast on 32 (34, 36, 38) sts.

Row 1 (WS): K14 (15, 16, 17), p4, k14 (15, 16, 17).

Row 2 (RS): K13 (14, 15, 16), p1, k4, p1, k13 (14, 15, 16).

Rows 3 and 4: Rep Rows 1 and 2.

Row 5: Rep Row 1.

Row 6: K13 (14, 15, 16), p1, C4B, p1, k13 (14, 15, 16).

Rows 7 and 8: Rep Rows 1 and 2.

Row 9: Rep Row 1.

Change to larger needles.

Body

Work in pat below, and *at the same time*, inc 1 st at each side edge [every 4th row] 6 (7, 5, 4) times, then [every 6th row] 2 (2, 5, 7) times, working inc sts into pat—48 (52, 56, 60) sts.

Row 1: K13 (14, 15, 16), p1, k4, p1, k13 (14, 15, 16).

Row 2: P13 (14, 15, 16), k1, p4, k1, p13 (14, 15, 16).

Row 3: K13 (14, 15, 16), p1, C4B, p1, k13 (14, 15, 16).

Row 4: Rep Row 2.

Row 5: Rep Row 1.

Row 6: K14 (15, 16, 17), p4, k14 (15, 16, 17).

Rep Rows 1–6 for pat.

When inc have been completed, work even in pat until piece measures 6 (6½, 7½, 8½) inches. Bind off all sts.

Finishing

Sew shoulder seams. Sew sleeves to body matching center sleeve cable to shoulder seam. Sew arm and side seams.

Neckband

With RS facing and smaller circular needle, beg at left shoulder seam, pick up and knit 9 sts along left front neck edge; knit across 16 (18, 20, 22) sts of front holder; pick up and knit 9 sts along right front edge to shoulder; pick up and knit 3 sts along right back neck edge; knit across 28 (30, 32, 34) sts of back holder; pick up and knit 3 sts along left back neck edge—68 (72, 76, 80) sts.

Join, marking beg of rnd.

Rnd 1: Purl around.

Rnd 2: Knit around.

Rnds 3 and 4: Rep Rnds 1 and 2.

Rnds 5–8: Work in k2, p2 rib.

Bind off loosely as to purl.

Hat

Border

With smaller circular needle, cast on 96 (108) sts. Join, being careful not to twist. Mark beg of rnd.

Rnd 1: Purl around.

Rnds 2–5: Work in k2, p2 rib.

Rnd 3: Knit around.

Rnd 4: Purl around.

Rnds 5 and 6: Rep Rnds 3 and 4.

Change to larger circular needle.

Body

Rnds 1, 2, 4 and 5: *K5 (6), p1, k4, p1, k5 (6); rep from * to end.

Rnd 3: *K5 (6), p1, C4B, p1, k5 (6); rep from * to end.

Rnd 6: *P6 (7), k4, p6 (7); rep from * to end.

Rep Rnds 1–6 until piece measures approx 3½ (4) inches, ending with Rnd 2 (6) of pat.

Shape crown
Note: Change to dpn as necessary.

For Large size only

Next rnd: *K5, p2tog-tbl, k4, p2tog, k5; rep from * to end—96 sts.

Next rnd: *K5, p1, k4, p1, k5; rep from * to end.

For Both sizes

Rnd 1: *K4, p2tog-tbl, C4B, p2tog, k4; rep from * to end—84 sts.

Rnds 2 and 3: *K4, p1, k4, p1, k4; rep from * to end.

Rnd 4: *P3, p2tog-tbl, k4, p2tog, p3; rep from * to end—72 sts.

Rnds 5 and 6: *K3, p1, k4, p1, k3; rep from * to end.

Rnd 7: *K2, p2tog-tbl, C4B, p2tog, k2; rep from * to end—60 sts.

Rnds 8 and 9: *K2, p1, k4, p1, k2; rep from * to end.

Rnd 10: *P1, p2tog-tbl, k4, p2tog, p1; rep from * to end—48 sts.

Rnds 11 and 12: *K1, p1, k4, p1, k1; rep from * to end.

Rnd 13: *P2tog-tbl, C4B, p2tog; rep from * to end—36 sts.

Rnds 14 and 15: *P1, k4, p1; rep from * to end.

Rnd 16: *K2tog, k2, ssk; rep from * to end—24 sts.

Rnd 17: Knit around.

Rnd 18: *Ssk, k2tog; rep from * to end—12 sts.

Cut yarn and draw through sts on needle twice.

Ear Flaps
Make 2

With smaller needle, cast on 13 (15) sts.

Knit 10 rows.

Continue in garter st (knit every row), and *at the same time*, dec 1 st at beg of next 10 (12) rows—3 sts.

I-cord tie
Make 2

*K3, sl sts to left needle, pull yarn across back of work; rep from * until cord measures 9 inches. K3tog. Fasten off.

Sew flaps to opposite sides of hat just under the ribbing.

Booties

Leg
With smaller needle, cast on 30 (38) sts.

Row 1 (WS): Knit.

Rows 2, 4 and 6: P2, *k2, p2; rep from * to end.

Rows 3 and 5: K2, *p2, k2; rep from * to end.

Row 7: Knit.

Row 8 (eyelet row): K2 (3), *yo, k2tog, k3 (4); rep from * to last 3 (5) sts, yo, k2tog, k1 (3).

Row 9: Knit.

Change to larger needles.

Rows 10, 14, 16 and 20: [P2, k2] 2 (3) times, k4, p1, k4, p1, k4, [k2, p2] 2 (3) times.

Rows 11, 13, 17 and 19: [K2, p2] 2 (3) times, p4, k1, p4, k1, p4, [p2, k2] 2 (3) times.

Rows 12 and 18: [P2, k2] 2 (3) times, k4, p1, C4B, p1, k4, [k2, p2] 2 (3) times.

Rows 15 and 21: [K2, p2] 1 (2) times, k9, p4, k9, [p2, k2] 1 (2) times.

Instep
Row 1: K12 (16), p1, k4, p1, k3 (4), turn.

Rows 2, 4, 8, 10: P3 (4), k1, p4, k1, p3 (4), turn.

Rows 3, 9: K3 (4), p1, C4B, p1, k3 (4), turn.

Rows 5, 7, 11: K3 (4), p1, k4, p1, k3 (4), turn.

Rows 6, 12: K4 (5), p4, k4 (5), turn.

For Large size only

Rep Rows 7–12.

Foot
For Both sizes
Row 1: K3 (4), p1, k4, p1, k3 (4), pick up 6 (9) sts along left side of instep, k9 (12), turn.

Row 2: P18 (25), k1, p4, k1, p3 (4), pick up 6 (9) sts from the WS along RS of instep, p9 (12)—42 (56) sts.

Row 3: K18 (25), p1, C4B, p1, k18 (25).

Rows 4–8: Knit.

Row 9: K1, k2tog, k13 (20), ssk, k6, k2tog, k13 (20), ssk, k1—38 (52) sts.

Rows 10, 12, 14: Knit.

Row 11: K1, k2tog, k11 (18), ssk, k6, k2tog, k11 (18), ssk, k1—34 (48) sts.

Row 13: K1, k2tog, k10 (17), ssk, k4, k2tog, k10 (17), ssk, k1—30 (44) sts.

Row 15: K1, k2tog, k8 (15), ssk, k4, k2tog, k8 (15), ssk, k1—26 (40) sts.

Bind off all sts knitwise.

Sew seam down back of leg and across bottom of sole.

I-cord tie
With smaller needle, cast on 2 sts.

*K2, sl 2 sts back to LH needle, pull yarn across back of work; rep from * until cord measures 15 inches. K2tog. Fasten off. Weave through eyelet row of bootie.

Afghan
With smaller needle, cast on 148 (220) sts.

Lower Border
Rows 1, 3, 5, 7, 9 (WS): K17, p6, *k30, p6; rep from * to last 17 sts, k17.

Rows 2, 6, 8 (RS): K16, p1, k6, p1, *k28, p1, k6, p1; rep from * to last 16 sts, k16.

Row 4: K16, p1, C6B, p1, *k28, p1, C6B, p1; rep from * to last 16 sts, k16.

Change to larger needle.

Body
Row 1 (RS): K16, p1, k6, p1, *k28, p1, k6, p1; rep from * to last 16 sts, k16.

Rows 2: K5, P11, k1, p6, k1, *p28, k1, p6, k1; rep from * to last 16 sts, p11, k5.

Row 3: K16, p1, C6B, p1, *k28, p1, C6B, p1; rep from * to last 16 sts, k16.

Row 4: Rep Row 2

Rows 5 and 6: Rep Rows 1 and 2.

Row 7: K5, p12, k6, *p30, k6; rep from * to last 17 sts, p12, k5.

Row 8: Rep Row 2.

Rep Rows 1–8 until piece measures approx 29 (39) inches, or to desired length, ending with Row 5 of pat.

Change to smaller needle.

Upper Border
Rep Rows 7–9 of lower border, then rep Rows 2–7.

Bind off all sts loosely. ❖

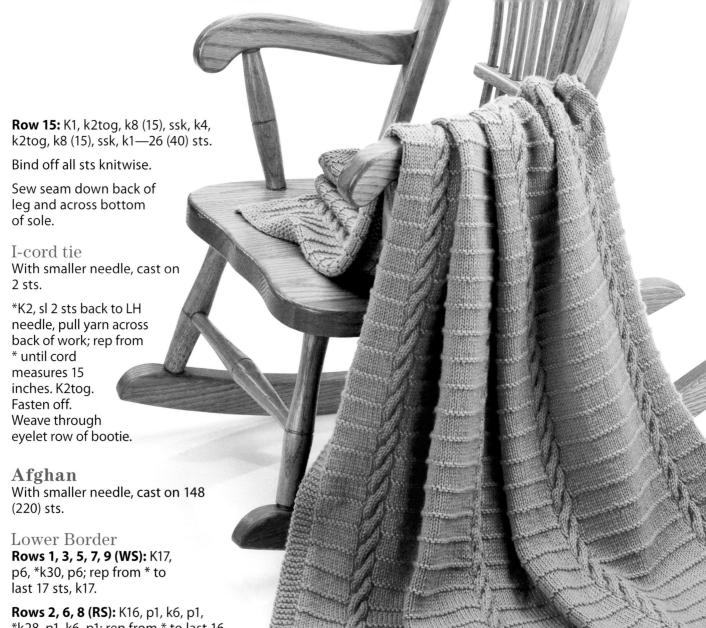

Little Dimples Layette

Designs by Kennita Tully

Skill Level
◼◼◼◻ INTERMEDIATE

Size
Infant's 6 (12, 18) months Instructions are given for smallest size, with larger sizes in parentheses. When only 1 number is given, it applies to all sizes.

Finished Measurements
Blanket: Approx 30 inches square
Sweater Chest: 22 (24, 26) inches
Sweater Length: 11 (12, 13) inches

Materials
• Plymouth Jeannee Worsted 51% cotton/49% acrylic worsted weight yarn (110 yds/50g per ball): 11 balls mint #18 for Blanket; 5 (5, 6) balls mint #18 for Sweater and Hat
• Size 8 (5mm) 16- and 36-inch circular needles or size needed to obtain gauge
• Tapestry needle
• Stitch holders

4 MEDIUM

Gauge
16 sts and 25 rows = 4 inches/10cm in Little Dimples pat. To save time, take time to check gauge.

Special Abbreviation
Increase (inc): Inc by knitting in front and back of next st.

Pattern Stitches
Little Dimple (for blanket)
Row 1 (RS): K1, inc in each st across to last st, k1.
Row 2: Purl across.
Row 3: Knit across.
Rows 4–7: [Rep Rows 2 and 3] twice.
Row 8: Rep Row 2.
Row 9: K1,*k2tog; rep from * to last st, k1.
Rows 10–14: Knit.
Rep Rows 1–14 for pat.

Little Dimples (for sweater and hat)
Row 1 (RS): K1, inc in each st across to last st, k1.
Row 2: Purl across.
Row 3: Knit across.
Rows 4 and 5: Rep Rows 2 and 3.
Row 6: Rep Row 2.
Row 7: K1, *k2tog; rep from * to last st, k1.
Rows 8–10: Knit.
Rep Rows 1–10 for pat.

Pattern Notes
Sweater is worked from side to side.
Different instructions are given for the pattern starting points on the body section to balance the pattern in the sweater body.
Work increases along back neck and front neck in the 4th stitch from the edge to keep the neckline from fluting.

Blanket
Cast on 120 sts.

Knit 8 rows.

Work [Rows 1–14 of Little Dimple pat for blanket] 15 times.

Knit 2 more rows.

Bind off all sts.

Finishing
Weave in all ends.

Sweater

Left Sleeve
Cast on 22 (24, 26) sts.

Knit 4 rows.

Work Rows 1–10 of Little Dimple pat for sweater.

Change to St st and inc each edge of next RS row, then [every RS row] 5 (3, 3) times, then [every 6th (4th, 4th) row] 3 (6, 7) times—40 (44, 48) sts.

Work even until sleeve measures approx 7 (7½, 8) inches, ending with a WS row.

Body
Continue in St st using knit or cable cast on, cast on 24 (26, 28) sts at beg next 2 rows—88 (96, 104) sts.

For 6 (18) month sizes only
Work 4 rows in St st.

Continue with For all sizes below.

For 12 month size only
Knit 4 rows.

Continue with For all sizes below.

For All sizes
Change to Little Dimple pat and beg with Row 7 (1) work in pat until body measures approx 2¾ (3¼, 3¾) inches ending by working Row 8.

Divide for back & front
Work in pat across 44 (48, 52) sts, place rem sts on holder for front.

Back
Working on back sts only, continue in pat until back measures approx 8¼ (8¾, 9¼) inches ending by working Row 8. Cut yarn and place these sts on a holder.

Front
Place front sts on needle and beg with RS row, bind off 4 sts at beg of row.

Continue in pat, dec 1 st at neck edge [every RS row] 5 times—35 (39, 43) sts.

Work even in pat for approx 3 inches ending by working a Row 6 of pat. Beg on next row inc 1 st at neck edge [each RS row] 5 times. Work 1 WS row, then cast on 4 sts at beg next RS row—44 (48, 52) sts.

Work 2 rows even and place sts on holder.

Join front & back
Transfer back sts to needle and work across back sts, then front sts now on a holder to join. Continue in pat across all sts until back measures approx 11 (12, 13) inches, ending by working a Row 4 (8, 4).

Right Sleeve
For 6 (18) month sizes only
Work 2 rows in st st.

Continue with For all sizes below.

For 12 month size only
Work 2 rows in garter st.

Continue with For all sizes below.

For All sizes
Working in St st (garter, St st), bind off 24 (26, 28) sts at beg next 2 rows.

Working in St st for all sizes, dec 1 st each edge [every 6th (4th, 4th) row] 3 (6, 7) times, then [every other row] 6 (4, 4) times—22 (24, 26) sts.

Knit 4 rows.

Rep Rows 1–10 of Little Dimple pat.

Bind off all sts.

Finishing
Wash and block pieces to measurements. Sew underarm and side seams.

Neckband
With smaller circular needle, pick up and knit 22 (24, 26) sts along back neck, 4 sts along bound-off sts, 24 sts along center front, 4 sts along bound-off sts—56 sts.

Join and work garter st in rnds (purl 1 rnd, knit 1 rnd) for 5 rows.

Bind off all sts loosely as to knit.

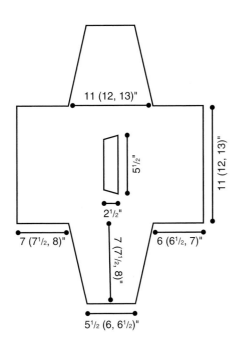

11 (12, 13)"

11 (12, 13)"

5½"

2½"

7 (7½, 8)"

7 (7½, 8)"

6 (6½, 7)"

5½ (6, 6½)"

Hat
Border
Cast on 72 sts.

Knit 4 rows.

Work Rows 1–10 of Little Dimple pat.

Body
Work in St st until hat measures 5 inches from cast-on edge.

Shape crown
Row 1: K1, *k8, k2 tog, rep from * to last st, end k1.

Rows 2, 4, 6 and all even-numbered rows: Purl across.

Row 3: K1, *k7, k2 tog; rep from * to last st, end k1.

Row 5: K1, *k6, k2 tog; rep from * to last st, end k1.

Continue in same manner, working 1 st less between dec until 16 sts rem.

Next row: K1, *k2 tog; rep from * across to last st, k1.

Cut yarn leaving an 18-inch end, draw through sts on needle twice. Sew seam. Weave in all ends. ❖

Tulip-Bud Jacket, Hat & Blanket

Designs by Sandi Prosser

Skill Level

■■■□ INTERMEDIATE

Sizes

Newborn–3 months (3–6 months, 6–12 months, 18–24 months) Instructions are given for smallest size, with larger sizes in parentheses. When only 1 number is given it applies to all sizes.

Finished Measurements

Chest: 19 (21, 23½, 25½) inches
Jacket Length: 11 (12, 13, 14) inches
Standard Blanket: Approx 40 inches square
Car-Seat Blanket: Approx 30 inches square

Materials

- Wendy Peter Pan DK Prints 55% nylon/45% acrylic DK weight yarn (186 yds/50g per ball): 3 (3, 4, 4) balls tropical crush #993 for Jacket; 1 (1, 1, 1) ball tropical crush #993 for Hat; 12 balls tropical crush #993 for standard Blanket and 7 balls tropical crush #993 for Car-Seat Blanket
- Size 3 (3.25mm) needles
- Size 6 (4.00mm) straight and 32-inch circular knitting needles or size needed to obtain gauge
- Size D/3 (3.25mm) crochet hook
- 3 buttons

Gauge

24 sts and 42 rows = 4 inches/10cm in garter st on larger needle.
To save time, take time to check gauge.

Special Abbreviation

Slip, knit, pass (skp): Sl next st as to purl, knit next st, pass slipped st over knit st.

Pattern Stitch

Tulip (worked over 33 sts)
Row 1 (WS): K16, p1, k16.
Row 2: K14, k2tog, yo, k1, yo, skp, k14.
Row 3: K14, p5, k14.
Row 4: K13, k2tog, yo, k3, yo, skp, k13.

Row 5: K13, p7, k13.
Row 6: K12, [k2tog, yo] twice, k1, [yo, skp] twice, k12.
Row 7: K12, p9, k12.
Row 8: K11, [k2tog, yo] twice, k3, [yo, skp] twice, k11.
Row 9: K11, p4, k1, p1, k1, p4, k11.
Row 10: K10, [k2tog, yo] twice, k5, [yo, skp] twice, k10.
Row 11: K10, p4, k2, p1, k2, p4, k10.
Row 12: K9, [k2tog, yo] twice, k3, yo, k1, yo, k3, [yo, skp] twice, k9—35 sts.
Row 13: K9, p4, k3, p3, k3, p4, k9.
Row 14: K1, yo, skp, k5, [k2tog, yo] twice, k5, yo, k1, yo, k5, [yo, skp] twice, k5, k2tog, yo, k1—37 sts.
Row 15: K1, p2, k5, p4, k4, p5, k4, p4, k5, p2, k1.
Row 16: K2, yo, skp, k3, [k2tog, yo] twice, k7, yo, k1, yo, k7, [yo, skp] twice, k3, k2tog, yo, k12—39 sts.
Row 17: K2, p2, k3, p4, k5, p7, k5, p4, k3, p2, k2.
Row 18: K3, yo, skp, k1, [k2tog, yo] twice, k9, yo, k1, yo, k9, [yo, skp] twice, k1, k2tog, yo, k3—41 sts.
Row 19: K3, p2, k1, p4, k6, p9, k6, p4, k1, p2, k3.
Row 20: K4, yo, sk2p, yo, k2tog, yo, k7, skp, k5, k2tog, k7, yo, skp, yo, k3tog, yo, k4—43 sts.
Row 21: K4, p5, k7, p7, k7, p5, k4.
Row 22: K16, skp, k3, k2tog, k16—37 sts.
Row 23: K16, p5, k16.
Row 24: K16, skp, k1, k2tog, k16—35 sts.
Row 25: K16, p3, k16.
Row 26: K16, sk2p, k16—33 sts.
Row 27 (WS): K16, p1, k16.

Jacket

Back

With larger needles, cast on 57 (63, 71, 77) sts.

Rows 1 (WS)–6: Knit.

Set up pat

Row 1 (WS): K12 (15, 19, 22), work Row 1 of Tulip pat, k12 (15, 19, 22).

Row 2: K12 (15, 19, 22), work Row 2 of Tulip pat, k12 (15, 19, 22).

Row 3: K12 (15, 19, 22), work Row 3 of Tulip pat, k12 (15, 19, 22).

Continue in pat as established until Row 27 of Tulip pat is completed.

Work even in garter st until piece measures 10½ (11½, 12½, 13½) inches from beg ending by working a WS row.

Shoulder & neck shaping
Next row (RS): K17 (19, 23, 25), join a 2nd ball of yarn and bind off center 23 (25, 25, 27) sts, knit to end of row.

Working both sides at once, bind off 2 sts at neck edge once—15 (17, 21, 23) sts.

Work even until piece measures 11 (12, 13, 14) inches, ending by working a WS row.

Bind off all sts.

Right Front
With larger needles, cast on 35 (37, 41, 43) sts.

Rows 1 (WS)–6: Knit.

Set up pat

Row 1 (WS): K1 (2, 4, 5), work Row 1 of Tulip pat, k1 (2, 4, 5).

Row 2: K1 (2, 4, 5), work Row 2 of Tulip pat, k1 (2, 4, 5).

Row 3: K1 (2, 4, 5), work Row 3 of Tulip pat, k1 (2, 4, 5).

Continue in pat as established until Row 27 of Tulip pat is completed.

Work even in garter st until piece measures 5¾ (6¾, 7¾, 8¾) inches from beg, ending by working a WS row.

Buttonhole row (RS): K3, yo, k2tog, knit to end of row.

Knit 11 rows.

Rep last 12 rows, then rep buttonhole row.

Work even until piece measures 9 (10, 11, 12) inches from beg, ending by working a WS row.

Neck shaping
Next row (RS): Bind off 12 sts, knit to end of row—23 (25, 29, 31) sts.

Work 1 row even then dec 1 st at neck edge of next and [every row] 7 times—15 (17, 21, 23) sts.

Work even sts until piece measures 11 (12, 13, 14) inches, ending by working a WS row.

Bind off all sts.

Left Front

With larger needles, cast on 35 (37, 41, 43) sts.

Rows 1 (WS)–6: Knit.

Set up pat

Row 1 (WS): K1 (2, 4, 5), work Row 1 of Tulip pat, k1 (2, 4, 5).

Row 2: K1 (2, 4, 5), work Row 2 of Tulip pat, k1 (2, 4, 5).

Row 3: K1 (2, 4, 5), work Row 3 of Tulip pat, k1 (2, 4, 5).

Continue in pat as established until Row 27 of Tulip pat is completed.

Work even in garter st until piece measures 9 (10, 11, 12) inches from beg, ending by working a RS row.

Neck shaping

Next row (WS): Bind off 12 sts, knit to end of row—23 (25, 29, 31) sts.

Work 1 row even then dec 1 st at neck edge of next and [every row] 7 times—15 (17, 21, 23) sts.

Work even sts until piece measures 11 (12, 13, 14) inches, ending by working a WS row.

Bind off all sts.

Sleeves

With larger needles, cast on 38 (40, 40, 42) sts. Work in garter st until piece measures 2 inches, noting that the first row is a WS row.

Inc 1 st at each end of next and [every 6th row] 4 (6, 8, 9) times—48 (54, 58, 62) sts.

Work even in garter st until piece measures 6 (6½, 8, 9½) inches, ending by working a WS row.

Bind off.

Finishing

Sew shoulder seams. Sew in sleeves. Sew side and sleeve seams. Sew buttons to left front to correspond to buttonholes.

Sleeve edging

Row 1: With RS facing and crochet hook, sc evenly around cast on edge of sleeve; join with sl st to first sc. Do not turn.

Row 2: Working from left to right, reverse sc in each sc to end of rnd; join with sl st to first st. Fasten off.

Jacket edging

Row 1: With RS facing and crochet hook, row sc

evenly around entire jacket edge, working 3 sc in each corner st; join with a sl st to first sc. Do not turn.

Row 2: Working from left to right, reverse sc in each sc around; join with a sl st to first st. Fasten off.

Hat

With smaller needles, cast on 92 (98, 104, 110) sts. Work in garter st for 5 rows, noting that the first row is a WS row.

Set up pat

Row 1 (RS): K5 (2, 5, 2), *yo, skp, k5, k2tog, yo, k3; rep from * to last 3 (0, 3, 0) sts, k3 (0, 3, 0).

Row 2: K3 (0, 3, 0), *k3, p2, k5, p2; rep from * to last 5 (2, 5, 2) sts, k5 (2, 5, 2).

Row 3: K5 (2, 5, 2), *k1, yo, skp, k3, k2tog, yo, k4; rep from * to last 3 (0, 3, 0) sts, k3 (0, 3, 0).

Row 4: K3 (0, 3, 0), *k4, p2, k3, p2, k1; rep from * to last 5 (2, 5, 2) sts, k5 (2, 5, 2).

Row 5: K5 (2, 5, 2), *k2, yo, skp, k1, k2tog, k5; rep from * to last 3 (0, 3, 0) sts, k3 (0, 3, 0).

Row 6: K3 (0, 3, 0), *k5, p2, k1, p2, k2; rep from * to last 5 (2, 5, 2) sts, k5 (2, 5, 2).

Row 7: K5 (2, 5, 2), *k3, yo, sk2p, yo, k6; rep from * to last 3 (0, 3, 0) sts, k3 (0, 3, 0).

Row 8: K3 (0, 3, 0), *k6, p3, k3; rep from * to last 5 (2, 5, 2) sts, k5 (2, 5, 2).

Continue even in garter st until piece measures 4 (4½, 5, 5½) inches, ending by working a WS row.

Top shaping

Next row (RS): K1, *k2tog, k11 (12, 13, 14), skp; rep from * to last st, k1—80 (86, 92, 98) sts.

Work 1 row even.

Next row: K1, *k2tog, k9 (10, 11, 12), skp; rep from * to last st—68 (74, 80, 86) sts.

Continue in same manner dec every RS row, until 20 (26, 20, 26) sts rem.

Next row (RS): K1, *k2tog; rep from * to last st, k1—11 (14, 11, 14) sts.

Break yarn, thread through rem sts, draw up tightly and fasten off securely. Sew center back seam.

Standard Blanket

Block 1
Make 36

With larger needles, cast on 3 sts.

Row 1 (RS): K1, inc, k1.

Row 2: K1, inc, knit to end of row.

Rep Row 2 until there are 44 sts.

Next row: K1, k2tog, knit to end of row.

Rep last row until 3 sts rem.

Bind off.

Finishing
Sew Block 1 squares tog following Assembly Diagram for blanket and directional lines.

Side strip
With circular needle, pick up and knit 185 evenly along 1 side of blanket.

Rows 1, 3 and 5 (WS): Knit.

Rows 2, 4 and 6: K1, inc, knit to last 3 sts, inc, k2.

Row 7: K14, work Row 1 of Tulip pat, [k29, work Row 1 of Tulip pat] twice, k14.

Row 8: K1, inc, k12, work Row 2 of Tulip pat, [k29, work Row 2 of Tulip pat] twice, k11, inc, k2.

Continue in pat as established, inc 1 st at each end of every RS row and working Tulip pat until Row 27 is complete.

Next row (RS): K1, inc, knit to last 3 sts, inc, k2.

Next row: Knit.

Rep [last 2 rows] twice more—223 sts.

Bind off all sts as to knit.

Rep side strip on rem 3 sides.

Sew miter corners tog.

Blanket edging
Row 1: With RS facing and crochet hook, sc evenly around entire blanket, working 3 sc in each corner, join with a sl st to first sc. Do not turn.

Row 2: Working from left to right, reverse sc in each sc around, join with a sl st to first st. Fasten off.

Car-Seat Blanket

Block 1
Make 16

With larger needles, cast on 3 sts.

Row 1 (RS): K1, inc, k1.

Row 2: K1, inc, knit to end of row.

Rep Row 2 until there are 44 sts on needle.

Next row: K1, k2tog, knit to end of row.

Rep last row until 3 sts rem.

Bind off.

Finishing
Sew Block 1 squares tog following Assembly Diagram 2 and directional arrows.

Side strip
With circular needle, pick up and knit 123 sts evenly along 1 side of blanket.

Rows 1, 3 and 5 (WS): Knit.

Rows 2, 4 and 6: K1, inc, knit to last 3 sts, inc, k2.

Row 7: K14, work Row 1 of Tulip pat, k29, work Row 1 of Tulip pat, k14.

Row 8: K1, inc, k12, work Row 2 of Tulip pat, k29, work Row 2 of Tulip pat, k11, inc, k2.

Continue in pat as established, inc at each end of every RS row and working Tulip pat until Row 27 is completed.

Next row (RS): K1, inc, knit to last 3 sts, inc, k2.

Next row: Knit.

Rep [last 2 rows] twice more—161 sts.

Bind off all sts as to knit.

Rep side strip on rem 3 sides.

Sew miter corners tog.

Car-Seat Blanket edging
Row 1: With RS facing and crochet hook, sc evenly around entire blanket, working 3 sc in each corner, join with a sl st to first sc. Do not turn.

Row 2: Working from left to right, reverse sc in each sc around; join with a sl st to first st. Fasten off. ❖

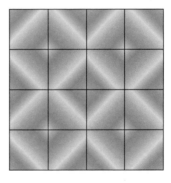

Tulip-Bud Jacket, Hat & Blanket
Assembly Diagram
Car-Seat Blanket

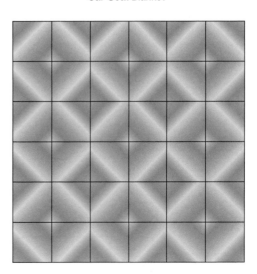

Tulip-Bud Jacket, Hat & Blanket
Assembly Diagram
Standard Blanket

Cuddly Cable Layette

Designs by Helen Stenborg

Skill Level
 INTERMEDIATE

Materials
- Schoeller + Stahl Popcorn 89% cotton/11% nylon bulky weight yarn (104 yds/50g per ball): 11 balls mint #16
- Size 4 (3.5mm) straight needles
- Size 8 (5mm) 29-inch circular and double-pointed needles or size needed to obtain gauge
- Stitch markers
- Stitch holders
- Cable needle
- Tapestry needle
- Size G/6 (4mm) crochet hook

Gauge
14 sts = 4 inches/10cm in cable pat with larger needles. To save time, take time to check gauge.

Special Abbreviations
Increase (inc): Inc by knitting in front and back of next st.

Cable Back (CB): Sl next 2 sts to cable needle and hold in back of work, k2, k2 from cable needle.

Pattern Stitches
Seed Stitch
Row/Rnd 1: *K1, p1, rep from * across.
Row/Rnd 2: Purl the knit sts and knit the purl sts.
Rep Row/Rnd 2 for pat.

Cable (multiple of 8 sts)
Note: To work in rnds: Knit all even-numbered cable pat rows instead of purling.
Row 1 (RS): Knit across.
Rows 2, 4 and 6: Purl across.
Row 3: *K4, CB; rep from * across.
Row 5: Knit across.
Row 7: *CB, k4; rep from * across.
Row 8: Rep Row 2.
Rep Rows 1–8 for pat.

Pattern Notes
Yarn amount given will make entire set. Blanket alone requires approximately 4 balls.
Circular needle used to accommodate number of stitches; do not join. Work back and forth in rows.

Blanket

Finished Size
Approx 27 x 44 inches

Instructions
With larger circular needle, cast on 100 sts and work in Seed St pat for 6 rows.

Beg pat

Next row (RS): Work Seed St pat across first 6 sts, place marker, work in Cable pat to last 6 sts, place marker, work rem sts in Seed St pat.

Continue to work in established pats until blanket measures 43 inches or 1 inch less than desired length.

Work 6 rows in Seed St pat. Bind off in pat.

Sweater

Size
Newborn–6 months

Finished Measurement
Chest: 20 inches

Hood

Hood edging
Beg at front edge with smaller needles, cast on 64 sts.

Rows 1 (RS) and 2: *K1, p1; rep from * across.

Row 3 (eyelet row): K1, p1, yo, k2tog, work in established K1, P1 rib to last 4 sts, k2tog, yo, k1, p1.

Rows 4–6: Continue in K1, P1 rib as established.

Change to larger circular needle.

Hood body

Row 1 (RS): Work 4 sts in Seed St pat, place marker, work Row 1 of Cable pat across to last 4 sts, place marker, work rem sts in Seed St pat.

Continue to work in pats as established with first and last 4 sts in Seed St pat and Cable pat between markers, and *at the same time,* work an eyelet row as above every 1½ inches until piece measures 7½ inches from beg.

Divide sts evenly on 2 needles dpns and work back seam using 3-needle bind off.

Yoke

With RS facing, pick up and knit 48 sts evenly around lower edge of hood. Purl 1 row.

Set up pat

Row 1 (RS): Work Seed St pat across 4 sts, k4, place marker, CB, k4, place marker, [CB, k4] twice, place marker, CB, k4, place marker, CB, work Seed St pat across rem 4 sts.

Row 2: Work Seed St pat across 4 sts, purl to last 4 sts, work Seed St pat across last 4 sts.

Row 3: Work Seed St pat across 4 sts, k3, inc, sl marker, inc, k6, inc, sl marker, inc, k14, inc, sl marker, inc, k6, inc, sl marker, inc, k3, work Seed St pat across last 4 sts.

Row 4: Work Seed St pat across 4 sts, purl to last 4 sts, work Seed St pat across last 4 sts.

Continuing to inc in this manner maintaining Seed St pat borders and Cable pat, working new sts into pat until there are 144 sts on needle. Yoke should measure approx 5½ inches from neck edge. Remove markers on last WS row.

Divide for body & sleeves

With RS facing, work in established pat across 20 sts, place next 32 sts on holder for sleeve, work across 40 back sts, place next 32 sts on holder for other sleeve, work last 20 sts.

Work in established pat on 80 body sts until piece measures 5 inches from underarm.

Work 5 rows Seed St pat, bind off in pat.

Sleeves

Divide sleeve sts onto dpns, join and work in rnds until sleeve measures 5 inches from underarm.

Dec 5 sts evenly around and work 5 rnds Seed St pat for cuff. Bind off all sts in pat.

Rep for other sleeve.

Tie

With crochet hook, crochet a 28-inch chain. Weave chain through eyelets and tie in a bow.

Booties

Finished Measurement
Foot: Approximately 4 inches

Instructions
Beg at bottom with larger needles, cast on 25 sts.

Row 1: K11, place marker, k3, place marker, k11.

Row 2: Knit across.

Row 3: Inc, work to 1 st before marker, inc, sl marker, k3, sl marker, inc, knit to end, inc in last st—29 sts.

Row 4: Knit across.

Rows 5 and 6: Rep Rows 3 and 4—33 sts.

Row 7: Knit to 1 st before marker, inc, sl marker, k3, sl marker, inc, knit to end.

Row 8: Purl.

Rows 9 and 10: Rep Rows 7 and 8—37 sts.

Shape toe
Row 1 (RS): Knit to 3 sts before marker, sl 1, k2tog, psso, sl marker, k3, sl marker, k3tog, knit to end—33 sts.

Row 2: Purl.

Rows 3–10: [Rep Rows 1 and 2] 4 times—17 sts.

Cuff
Work 6 rows of Seed St pat. Bind off in pat.

Sew seam. ❖

METRIC CONVERSION CHARTS

METRIC CONVERSIONS

yards	x	.9144	=	metres (m)
yards	x	91.44	=	centimetres (cm)
inches	x	2.54	=	centimetres (cm)
inches	x	25.40	=	millimetres (mm)
inches	x	.0254	=	metres (m)

centimetres	x	.3937	=	inches
metres	x	1.0936	=	yards

INCHES INTO MILLIMETRES & CENTIMETRES (Rounded off slightly)

inches	mm	cm	inches	cm	inches	cm	inches	cm
1/8	3	0.3	5	12.5	21	53.5	38	96.5
1/4	6	0.6	5 1/2	14	22	56	39	99
3/8	10	1	6	15	23	58.5	40	101.5
1/2	13	1.3	7	18	24	61	41	104
5/8	15	1.5	8	20.5	25	63.5	42	106.5
3/4	20	2	9	23	26	66	43	109
7/8	22	2.2	10	25.5	27	68.5	44	112
1	25	2.5	11	28	28	71	45	114.5
1 1/4	32	3.2	12	30.5	29	73.5	46	117
1 1/2	38	3.8	13	33	30	76	47	119.5
1 3/4	45	4.5	14	35.5	31	79	48	122
2	50	5	15	38	32	81.5	49	124.5
2 1/2	65	6.5	16	40.5	33	84	50	127
3	75	7.5	17	43	34	86.5		
3 1/2	90	9	18	46	35	89		
4	100	10	19	48.5	36	91.5		
4 1/2	115	11.5	20	51	37	94		

KNITTING NEEDLES CONVERSION CHART

Canada/U.S.	0	1	2	3	4	5	6	7	8	9	10	10½	11	13	15
Metric (mm)	2	2¼	2¾	3¼	3½	3¾	4	4½	5	5½	6	6½	8	9	10

CROCHET HOOKS CONVERSION CHART

Canada/U.S.	1/B	2/C	3/D	4/E	5/F	6/G	8/H	9/I	10/J	10½/K	N
Metric (mm)	2.25	2.75	3.25	3.5	3.75	4.25	5	5.5	6	6.5	9.0

STANDARD ABBREVIATIONS

[ ] work instructions within brackets as many times as directed

( ) work instructions within parentheses in the place directed

** repeat instructions following the asterisks as directed

* repeat instructions following the single asterisk as directed

" inch(es)

approx approximately

beg begin/beginning

CC contrasting color

ch chain stitch

cm centimeter(s)

cn cable needle

dec decrease/decreases/decreasing

dpn(s) double-pointed needle(s)

g gram

inc increase/increases/increasing

k knit

k2tog knit 2 stitches together

LH left hand

lp(s) loop(s)

m meter(s)

M1 make one stitch

MC main color

mm millimeter(s)

oz ounce(s)

p purl

pat(s) pattern(s)

p2tog purl 2 stitches together

psso pass slipped stitch over

p2sso pass 2 slipped stitches over

rem remain/remaining

rep repeat(s)

rev St st reverse stockinette stitch

RH right hand

rnd(s) rounds

RS right side

skp slip, knit, pass stitch over— one stitch decreased

sk2p slip 1, knit 2 together, pass slip stitch over the knit 2 together— 2 stitches have been decreased

sl slip

sl 1k slip 1 knitwise

sl 1p slip 1 purlwise

sl st slip stitch(es)

ssk slip, slip, knit these 2 stitches together—a decrease

st(s) stitch(es)

St st stockinette stitch/ stocking stitch

tbl through back loop(s)

tog together

WS wrong side

wyib with yarn in back

wyif with yarn in front

yd(s) yard(s)

yfwd yarn forward

yo yarn over

E-mail: Customer_Service@whitebirches.com

HOUSE of WHITE BIRCHES
PUBLISHERS SINCE 1947

Just for Baby is published by DRG, 306 East Parr Road, Berne, IN 46711, telephone (260) 589-4000. Printed in USA. Copyright © 2009 DRG. All rights reserved. This publication may not be reproduced in part or in whole without written permission from the publisher.

RETAIL STORES: If you would like to carry this pattern book or any other DRG publications, call the Wholesale Department at Annie's Attic to set up a direct account: (903) 636-4303. Also, request a complete listing of publications available from DRG.

Every effort has been made to ensure that the instructions in this pattern book are complete and accurate. We cannot, however, take responsibility for human error, typographical mistakes or variations in individual work.

STAFF

Editor: Jeanne Stauffer
Managing Editor: Dianne Schmidt
Technical Editor: Kathy Wesley
Technical Artist: Nicole Gage
Copy Supervisor: Michelle Beck
Copy Editors: Amanda Ladig, Mary O'Donnell
Graphic Arts Supervisor: Ronda Bechinski

Graphic Artists: Pam Gregory, Erin Augsburger
Art Director: Brad Snow
Assistant Art Director: Nick Pierce
Photography Supervisor: Tammy Christian
Photography: Matt Owen
Photo Stylist: Tammy Steiner

ISBN: 978-1-59217-242-9

3 4 5 6 7 8 9 10 11

Photo Index

14

10

24

18

7

28

12

16

20

2

44

34

4

38